Copyright © 2023 by Ryan P. Parker (Author)

All rights reserved. No part of this book may be reproduced or utilized in any form or by any means, electronic or mechanical, including photocopying, recording or by any information storage and retrieval system, without permission in writing from the publisher, except for brief quotations in critical articles or reviews.

The content of this book is based on various sources and is intended for educational and entertainment purposes only. While the author has made every effort to ensure the accuracy, completeness, and reliability of the information provided, the information may be subject to errors, omissions, or inaccuracies. Therefore, the author makes no warranties, express or implied, regarding the content of this book.

Readers are advised to seek the guidance of a licensed professional before attempting any techniques or actions outlined in this book. The author is not responsible for any losses, damages, or injuries that may arise from the use of information contained within. The information provided in this book is not intended to be a substitute for professional advice, and readers should not rely solely on the information presented.

By reading this book, readers acknowledge that the author is not providing legal, financial, medical, or professional advice. Any reliance on the information contained in this book is solely at the reader's own risk.

Thank you for selecting this book as a valuable source of knowledge and inspiration. Our aim is to provide you with insights and information that will enrich your understanding and enhance your personal growth. We appreciate your decision to embark on this journey of discovery with us, and we hope that this book will exceed your expectations and leave a lasting impact on your life.

Title: Injury, Triumph, and the Road Less Traveled
Subtitle: The Stories of Yannick Noah, Iva Majoli, and Marion Bartoli

Series: Sports Through Time: A Comprehensive History
Author: Ryan P. Parker

Table of Contents

Introduction **5**
Providing an overview of Book 2 and its focus on the unique journeys of Yannick Noah, Iva Majoli, and Marion Bartoli. 5
Highlighting the difficulties of maintaining top form and consistency in the tennis world. 8
Introducing Yannick Noah, Iva Majoli, and Marion Bartoli, setting the stage for their remarkable stories. 10

Chapter 1: Yannick Noah - The French Phenom **13**
Noah's Tennis Beginnings 13
Triumph at the French Open 1983 15
The Pressure to Maintain Success 17
Struggles with Injuries and the Pursuit of Top Form 19

Chapter 2: Iva Majoli - The Croatian Hope **21**
Majoli's Early Tennis Journey 21
French Open Victory at 19 23
The Challenges of Consistency 25
Battling Injuries and Maintaining Form 28

Chapter 3: Marion Bartoli - The Wimbledon Enigma
.... **31**
Bartoli's Tennis Origins 31
Remarkable Wimbledon Win in 2013 33
Health Issues and Injuries: A Constant Battle 35
The Determined Comebacks 37

Chapter 4: Overcoming Adversity **40**
How These Players Overcame Initial Hurdles 40
Noah's Resilience in the Face of Injuries 43

Majoli's Struggle for Consistency and Recovery *45*
Bartoli's Battle Against Health Issues *48*
Chapter 5: Life Beyond Tennis **51**
Yannick Noah's Post-Tennis Journey *51*
Iva Majoli's Career After the Courts *54*
Marion Bartoli's Impact and Pursuits Beyond Tennis *56*
Chapter 6: Legacy and Inspiration **59**
The Lasting Impact of These One Slam Wonders *59*
Lessons in Resilience and Determination *62*
Inspiring Future Generations *65*
Chapter 7: The Sporting World's Take **68**
Insights and Quotes from Tennis Professionals and Experts *68*
How These Players Are Remembered *71*
Examining the Cultural and Historical Significance *74*
Conclusion **77**
Reflecting on the Remarkable Journeys *77*
The Unique Legacy of Yannick Noah, Iva Majoli, and Marion Bartoli *80*
Celebrating Their Enduring Mark in Tennis History *83*
Wordbook **86**
Supplementary Materials **89**

Introduction
Providing an overview of Book 2 and its focus on the unique journeys of Yannick Noah, Iva Majoli, and Marion Bartoli.

In the world of tennis, where champions are often defined by the number of Grand Slam titles they accumulate, there exists a select group of individuals who stand out for a different reason. They are the players who, despite their immense talent and unwavering dedication, secured only a single Grand Slam victory throughout their careers. Yet, the narratives of these athletes are no less extraordinary than those of the multi-title winners. Their stories are tales of injury, triumph, and the courage to tread the road less traveled.

Welcome to "Injury, Triumph, and the Road Less Traveled," a compelling exploration of the careers and lives of three remarkable tennis players: Yannick Noah, Iva Majoli, and Marion Bartoli. In the pages that follow, we will journey through the annals of tennis history to uncover the unique challenges and achievements that define these three athletes.

Our quest begins with Yannick Noah, the charismatic French phenom who took the tennis world by storm in the early 1980s. His triumph at the 1983 French Open remains etched in the sport's history, but what followed was a rollercoaster ride of injuries and relentless pursuit of excellence.

Then, we turn our attention to Iva Majoli, the Croatian hope who clinched her first and only Grand Slam title at the tender age of 19. Majoli's journey is a testament to the challenges of consistency in an unforgiving sport, where every match demands excellence.

Lastly, we delve into the enigmatic world of Marion Bartoli, whose remarkable Wimbledon victory in 2013 surprised and inspired tennis fans worldwide. Her career was marred by health issues and injuries, but Bartoli's determination and comebacks remain an inspiration to all.

This book is not just a collection of their victories and defeats on the tennis court; it is a deep dive into the minds and hearts of these players. It's about the pressures they faced, the adversities they overcame, and the indomitable spirit that carried them through. It's about life beyond tennis and the lasting impact they've left on the sport.

So, join us as we embark on a journey through the lives of these one-slam wonders, a journey filled with triumphs, trials, and a profound appreciation for the road they chose to travel. In doing so, we hope to uncover the essence of what it truly means to be a champion, both on and off the court.

Highlighting the difficulties of maintaining top form and consistency in the tennis world.

The world of professional tennis is a relentless battleground, where the pursuit of excellence is relentless, and the margin between triumph and defeat can be as fine as the width of a tennis net. In this chapter, we delve deep into the challenges that every tennis player faces in their quest for glory, with a particular focus on the difficulties of maintaining top form and consistency.

The Unforgiving Nature of Tennis: Tennis is an unforgiving sport where each match demands peak physical and mental performance. The tennis calendar is a grueling one, with players crisscrossing the globe to compete in various tournaments. The physical toll of constant travel and competition can be draining, making it difficult to sustain top-level play.

The Mental Game: Tennis is not just a physical battle; it's also a mental one. Maintaining the right mindset and mental fortitude is crucial for success. The pressure to perform in front of thousands of spectators, the weight of expectations, and the scrutiny from fans and media can take a toll on even the most seasoned players.

Injuries and Recovery: Injuries are an inherent part of a tennis player's life. The intense physical demands of the sport make players susceptible to various injuries, from the wear and tear of joints to more acute injuries that can sideline them for weeks or even months. Recovering from injuries and returning to top form is a monumental challenge.

Consistency: The Holy Grail: In tennis, consistency is the holy grail that every player chases. It's not enough to have one outstanding match; champions must deliver exceptional performances consistently. Maintaining that level of play week in and week out is a monumental task that requires not only physical fitness but also mental resilience.

The Evolving Competition: The tennis landscape is constantly changing. New talents emerge, hungry to dethrone the established champions. Adapting to new styles of play, strategies, and opponents is a challenge that every player faces. Staying ahead of the curve is no small feat.

In the chapters that follow, we will see how Yannick Noah, Iva Majoli, and Marion Bartoli navigated these challenges on their individual journeys to Grand Slam victory. Their stories will shed light on the immense sacrifices, dedication, and determination required to achieve and maintain success in the world of tennis.

Introducing Yannick Noah, Iva Majoli, and Marion Bartoli, setting the stage for their remarkable stories.

Before we embark on the enthralling journeys of Yannick Noah, Iva Majoli, and Marion Bartoli, it's essential to get acquainted with these three remarkable individuals who have left an indelible mark on the world of tennis. Each of them possesses a unique background, a distinctive playing style, and a story that resonates with the hearts of tennis enthusiasts and fans worldwide.

Yannick Noah: The French Phenom

Our first protagonist, Yannick Noah, hails from the picturesque landscapes of France. With his charismatic charm and exceptional athleticism, he burst onto the tennis scene in the late 1970s and early 1980s, captivating fans with his prowess on the clay courts. Noah's journey is one of immense talent, staggering expectations, and a relentless pursuit of excellence. He etched his name in the annals of tennis history with a monumental victory at the French Open in 1983, becoming the first Frenchman in 37 years to win the prestigious tournament. But as we shall soon discover, the road to that historic triumph was fraught with challenges, injuries, and the daunting pressure to maintain success.

Iva Majoli: The Croatian Hope

Our second protagonist, Iva Majoli, emerged from the tennis-rich country of Croatia, where she began her journey in the sport at a young age. Her story is one of youthful promise and meteoric rise. At just 19 years old, Majoli clinched the French Open title, announcing herself as a force to be reckoned with in women's tennis. However, the path to sustained greatness proved to be a Herculean task. Consistency and recovery from injuries became her constant companions, testing her mettle and determination.

Marion Bartoli: The Wimbledon Enigma

Our third protagonist, Marion Bartoli, hails from France and made headlines with her unorthodox playing style and unmatched determination. She achieved her crowning glory at Wimbledon in 2013, a victory that took the tennis world by surprise and marked her as a true enigma of the sport. Yet, Bartoli's journey was filled with battles against health issues and injuries, transforming her into an inspiration for those who dare to overcome adversity.

As we delve deeper into their individual narratives, we will witness the triumphs, the tribulations, and the enduring spirit that define these three tennis icons. Their stories are not just about their achievements on the tennis court but also about the resilience of the human spirit in the face of overwhelming odds. Join us as we unravel the unique tapestries of their lives and celebrate the champions they are, both on and off the court.

Chapter 1: Yannick Noah - The French Phenom
Noah's Tennis Beginnings

The story of Yannick Noah's ascent to tennis stardom begins in the vibrant city of Sedan, nestled in the picturesque Ardennes region of France. Born on May 18, 1960, Yannick Noah was destined for greatness from an early age. His father, Zacharie Noah, himself a former professional footballer and a Cameroonian of great repute, instilled in young Yannick a love for sports and a determination to excel.

Noah's journey into the world of tennis commenced in the early 1970s when he picked up a tennis racket for the first time. It wasn't long before his natural athleticism and hand-eye coordination caught the attention of local coaches. His early days on the court were marked by boundless enthusiasm and a relentless work ethic, traits that would become the hallmarks of his tennis career.

At the age of 11, Noah moved to Paris to further his tennis education and to train under the watchful eye of French tennis coach Charlie Pasarell. It was in the heart of the French capital that he honed his skills, spending countless hours on the clay courts of the prestigious Racing Club de France. There, he developed a playing style characterized by a powerful serve, explosive forehand, and remarkable agility on the court.

Noah's first foray onto the international tennis scene came in the late 1970s when he competed in junior tournaments and began to garner attention for his prodigious talent. His charisma and distinctive dreadlocked hairstyle also made him a fan favorite, endearing him to tennis enthusiasts worldwide.

As Yannick Noah's skills matured, he quickly ascended the ranks of professional tennis. His journey from a young boy swinging a racket in Sedan to a rising star in the tennis world was marked by dedication, passion, and an unwavering belief in his abilities. Little did he know that this was just the beginning of a remarkable career that would ultimately culminate in one of the most significant achievements in the history of French tennis—a triumphant victory at the French Open in 1983.

Triumph at the French Open 1983

The year was 1983, and the stage was set at the hallowed grounds of Roland Garros, where the world's finest tennis players gathered to compete in the French Open. For Yannick Noah, this tournament represented the culmination of years of hard work, dedication, and a dream that had taken root in the clay courts of Sedan and blossomed under the Parisian sun.

As the tournament progressed, Noah's incredible journey through the draws was nothing short of spectacular. His powerful serve and athleticism on the clay courts left opponents in awe and fans on the edge of their seats. He faced formidable adversaries, including some of the era's most accomplished players, but his unwavering determination and fearless play saw him surmount each challenge.

The defining moment of Noah's 1983 French Open campaign came in the final, when he squared off against Mats Wilander, a rising Swedish star known for his prowess on clay. The match was a fierce battle of wills, a test of skill and mental fortitude. The crowd at Roland Garros, overwhelmingly French and fervently supportive of their compatriot, created an electric atmosphere that added to the drama on the court.

Noah's victory in that memorable final was a testament to his extraordinary talent and unwavering resolve. With each stroke of the racket and every point won, he inched closer to his dream of becoming a Grand Slam champion. When he finally secured the championship point, the roar of the crowd was deafening, and Yannick Noah dropped to his knees, tears of joy streaming down his face. He had not only achieved a personal milestone but had also etched his name in the annals of French tennis history.

The French Open victory of 1983 was a transformative moment not only for Yannick Noah but also for French tennis as a whole. He became the first Frenchman in 37 years to win the prestigious tournament, a feat that catapulted him to legendary status in his homeland. The triumph was a symbol of hope and inspiration for generations of aspiring tennis players in France, who saw in Noah's journey a reflection of their own dreams and aspirations.

As we delve deeper into Noah's life and career, we will uncover the pressures and challenges that followed his historic victory, as well as the enduring legacy he left in the world of tennis.

The Pressure to Maintain Success

Yannick Noah's victory at the French Open in 1983 was nothing short of a fairy tale come true. It was a moment that etched his name in the annals of tennis history and made him a national hero in France. However, with triumph came an entirely new set of challenges - the relentless pressure to maintain success.

As the first Frenchman in nearly four decades to win the French Open, Noah became an instant icon. The weight of expectations from his country and its passionate tennis fans bore down on him. Every match, every tournament became a high-stakes affair, with fans eagerly awaiting another victory to celebrate. The pressure to perform consistently at the highest level was immense.

Noah's playing style, characterized by flair and power, thrilled spectators. But it also meant that his game was heavily scrutinized. Tennis pundits and fans analyzed every aspect of his play, from his serves to his volleys, searching for any sign of weakness or vulnerability. Maintaining his physical and mental peak became a constant challenge, as the competition on the tour was fierce, and opponents were determined to dethrone the French champion.

Injuries added another layer of complexity to Noah's quest for continued success. The physical toll of professional tennis, with its grueling schedule and rigorous training regimens, took a toll on his body. Injuries and niggling health issues became a recurrent theme in his career, forcing him to withdraw from tournaments and impacting his performance.

The pressure to maintain success not only affected Noah's on-court performance but also seeped into his personal life. The demands of the sport meant he spent extensive time away from his family, leading to personal sacrifices and the challenge of balancing a high-profile career with his role as a father and husband.

In the pages that follow, we will delve deeper into Yannick Noah's career, exploring the highs and lows that followed his historic French Open triumph. We will witness his resilience in the face of adversity, his unrelenting pursuit of excellence, and the enduring legacy he left in the world of tennis. Noah's journey is not just a tale of tennis but a testament to the extraordinary pressures faced by those who reach the pinnacle of their sport and the determination required to stay there.

Struggles with Injuries and the Pursuit of Top Form

Yannick Noah's journey to maintain success in the tennis world was fraught with a formidable adversary: injuries. As he basked in the glory of his 1983 French Open victory, little did he know that the path ahead would be strewn with physical setbacks, testing his resolve and determination to the fullest.

Noah's playing style was built on power and agility, which had taken a toll on his body over the years. The relentless demands of the professional circuit and the unforgiving nature of the sport left him susceptible to a range of injuries. His battles with aching joints, strained muscles, and other tennis-related injuries became a recurring theme in his career.

Maintaining top form in the face of injuries proved to be an unceasing challenge. Time and again, Noah found himself sidelined, forced to withdraw from tournaments and undergo extensive rehabilitation. These periods of recuperation were frustrating, as he watched his ranking slip and his form wane. The pressure to perform at his best, even when not fully fit, weighed heavily on his shoulders.

The pursuit of top form became a relentless quest. Noah, known for his incredible work ethic, pushed himself to the limits in training and physical conditioning. He sought the expertise of medical professionals to manage his injuries and minimize their impact on his career. Each comeback from injury was a testament to his resilience and unwavering commitment to the sport he loved.

In these moments of adversity, Yannick Noah's mental fortitude shone brightly. He faced not only the physical pain of injuries but also the mental challenges of self-doubt and frustration. Yet, he emerged from each setback with renewed determination, using his setbacks as stepping stones to reach new heights.

As we explore Yannick Noah's struggles with injuries and his relentless pursuit of top form, we gain a deeper understanding of the character of this French phenom. His story is one of triumph over adversity, a testament to the enduring spirit of a champion who refused to be defined by setbacks. In the chapters that follow, we will witness his incredible comebacks and the indomitable will that made him an enduring figure in the world of tennis.

Chapter 2: Iva Majoli - The Croatian Hope
Majoli's Early Tennis Journey

Iva Majoli's remarkable journey in the world of tennis began in the picturesque coastal city of Zagreb, Croatia. Born on August 12, 1977, she was introduced to the sport at an early age by her parents, both of whom had a passion for tennis. Little did they know that their daughter's first swings of the racket would mark the genesis of an exceptional career.

At just five years old, Majoli started hitting tennis balls on the local courts with her father, Slobodan. Her innate talent and dedication quickly became apparent as she displayed an uncanny ability to strike the ball with precision and agility. Recognizing her potential, her parents enrolled her in a local tennis club, where her journey towards greatness officially began.

Iva Majoli's early years on the tennis court were marked by countless hours of practice and unwavering determination. She trained tirelessly, honing her skills and developing her unique playing style, which combined a powerful baseline game with a relentless work ethic. Her dedication was palpable, and she showed an unparalleled appetite for improvement.

As she progressed through the ranks of junior tennis in Croatia, Majoli's talent did not go unnoticed. Her remarkable success in junior tournaments brought her to the attention of tennis coaches and scouts, who recognized her as a rising star with the potential to make a significant impact on the professional circuit.

In 1992, at the age of 15, Iva Majoli made her professional debut on the WTA Tour. Her fearless play and composure on the court belied her young age, earning her respect and admiration from fellow competitors and fans alike. It was clear that she was destined for greatness, and her rapid ascent up the rankings confirmed her status as the Croatian hope in women's tennis.

As we delve deeper into Iva Majoli's early tennis journey, we will witness the sacrifices made by her and her family, the challenges she faced as a young prodigy, and the determination that propelled her towards her historic French Open victory at just 19 years old. Her story is a testament to the indomitable spirit of a young athlete who dared to dream big and worked tirelessly to turn those dreams into reality.

French Open Victory at 19

The year was 1997, and the prestigious clay courts of Roland Garros in Paris were set for one of the most unforgettable chapters in tennis history. Iva Majoli, the Croatian hope, entered the French Open at the tender age of 19, and what followed would become a testament to her unwavering determination and remarkable talent.

Majoli's journey through the draws of the 1997 French Open was nothing short of a revelation. Her fearless play, powerful groundstrokes, and unshakeable focus made her a formidable opponent for anyone who crossed her path. With each victory, her confidence grew, and the tennis world began to take notice.

In the final, Majoli faced none other than the legendary Swiss player Martina Hingis, a dominant force in women's tennis at the time. Hingis was the reigning world No. 1 and the overwhelming favorite to clinch the title. However, Majoli was undeterred by the odds stacked against her.

The final match was a grueling battle that showcased Majoli's remarkable grit and composure. She fought tirelessly, covering every inch of the court, and her powerful forehand and precise backhand found their mark repeatedly.

With each passing game, she inched closer to her dream of Grand Slam glory.

As the final point was secured, and the Roland Garros crowd erupted in applause, Iva Majoli dropped her racket and fell to her knees, tears of joy streaming down her face. She had achieved what many considered impossible—a victory over the formidable Martina Hingis in the final of the French Open.

The significance of Majoli's triumph cannot be overstated. She became the first Croatian woman to win a Grand Slam singles title, a momentous achievement that brought immense pride to her homeland. Her victory inspired a generation of young Croatian tennis players, who saw in her journey a reflection of their own dreams and aspirations.

Iva Majoli's French Open victory at 19 is a chapter etched in the history of tennis. It is a story of youthful determination, courage in the face of adversity, and the realization of a dream that few believed possible. As we delve deeper into her life and career, we will uncover the challenges that followed her historic triumph and the lasting impact she left on the world of tennis.

The Challenges of Consistency

Iva Majoli's French Open victory at the age of 19 was a crowning achievement, a moment when the tennis world took notice of her immense talent and determination. However, as she basked in the glory of her historic win, a new set of challenges emerged, chief among them the pursuit of consistency.

Consistency is the holy grail of professional tennis. It's the ability to deliver exceptional performances not just on the grand stages of Grand Slam tournaments but week in and week out on the tour. It's about maintaining a high level of play, regardless of the venue, the surface, or the opponent. And for Iva Majoli, this pursuit of consistency presented formidable hurdles.

The pressure that comes with being a Grand Slam champion is immense. The expectations are sky-high, and the spotlight shines even brighter. Every match, every tournament becomes a high-stakes affair, with fans and pundits eagerly awaiting her performances. Maintaining the mental fortitude to handle this constant scrutiny while striving for excellence was a significant challenge.

The physical demands of the professional tennis circuit also posed challenges. The rigorous travel schedule, the wear and tear on the body, and the relentless training regimens could be physically draining. Injuries, which had been a recurring theme in Majoli's career, added an additional layer of complexity to the quest for consistency. Finding the balance between pushing her limits and avoiding injury became a delicate dance.

Adapting to different playing conditions and opponents was another obstacle. Tennis is a sport with a wide variety of playing surfaces, each demanding a different set of skills and strategies. Maintaining a high level of play on both clay and hard courts, against power hitters and counter-punchers alike, required constant adaptation and learning.

Majoli's journey through the ups and downs of consistency is a testament to her resilience. She faced moments of triumph and moments of struggle, but through it all, she remained committed to the sport she loved. Her story is a reflection of the challenges that all professional tennis players face as they strive for excellence and the enduring spirit required to overcome them.

In the chapters that follow, we will delve deeper into Iva Majoli's career, exploring the battles she fought to maintain her form, the setbacks she encountered, and the determination that kept her on the path of greatness. Her journey is not just a tale of tennis but a testament to the pursuit of excellence in the face of adversity.

Battling Injuries and Maintaining Form

Iva Majoli's journey through the world of professional tennis was a relentless struggle against not only opponents on the court but also the physical challenges posed by injuries. Her career was punctuated by moments of brilliance and triumph, but it was also marked by periods of adversity and the daunting task of maintaining form in the face of physical setbacks.

Injuries, as in many sports, are an inevitable part of a tennis player's life. The repetitive strain on the body, the constant pivoting and sprinting, and the demands of an intense playing schedule make injuries an occupational hazard. For Majoli, these injuries were not just occasional inconveniences; they became recurring companions on her journey.

Perhaps one of the most challenging aspects of dealing with injuries in professional tennis is the mental toll they can take. The frustration of being sidelined, the uncertainty of recovery timelines, and the nagging doubts about one's ability to return to peak form can be emotionally draining. Maintaining mental resilience while facing physical setbacks is a formidable challenge for any athlete.

Majoli's battles with injuries often saw her withdraw from tournaments and undertake rigorous rehabilitation programs. These periods of forced rest and recovery tested her patience and resolve. Yet, she approached each setback with determination, working diligently with medical professionals to address the physical issues and regain her strength and mobility.

The pursuit of maintaining top form was not just about recovery from injuries but also about staying competitive. Tennis is a sport where a player's ranking is determined by consistent performances, and Majoli faced the daunting task of maintaining her position among the world's elite. The pressure to perform at a high level, even when not fully fit, was ever-present.

Despite the challenges, Iva Majoli's career is a testament to her perseverance. She displayed an unwavering commitment to her craft, working tirelessly to recover from injuries and return to the court. Her comebacks were not just about reclaiming her form but also about proving her resilience.

In the chapters that follow, we will delve deeper into Majoli's battles with injuries, exploring the physical and mental challenges she faced, and witnessing her determination to overcome adversity. Her story is a testament to the indomitable spirit of a true champion who refused to be defined by setbacks, ultimately leaving an enduring mark on the world of tennis.

Chapter 3: Marion Bartoli - The Wimbledon Enigma
Bartoli's Tennis Origins

Marion Bartoli's extraordinary journey in the world of tennis began in the picturesque city of Le Puy-en-Velay, France. Born on October 2, 1984, Bartoli was introduced to the sport at an early age, thanks in no small part to her tennis-loving family.

Her father, Walter Bartoli, a medical doctor with a passion for tennis, played a pivotal role in nurturing Marion's early interest in the sport. He became her coach, mentor, and biggest supporter, instilling in her a love for tennis and a work ethic that would set the foundation for her remarkable career.

Marion's unique playing style, marked by a two-handed forehand and backhand, was developed during her formative years. This unorthodox technique, often considered unconventional in the world of professional tennis, was a product of her father's coaching philosophy. It emphasized maximizing power and precision on both sides of the court.

Her early years were spent on the tennis courts of Le Puy-en-Velay, where she honed her skills and competed in local tournaments. Marion's dedication to the sport was evident from a young age, as she tirelessly practiced her strokes, improved her fitness, and harbored dreams of becoming a professional tennis player.

As Marion Bartoli's talent blossomed, her family recognized her potential and decided to take the bold step of moving to Paris to provide her with more extensive tennis training opportunities. The bustling capital city became the backdrop for the next chapter of her tennis journey.

In Paris, Bartoli's commitment to her craft deepened as she immersed herself in the competitive world of junior tennis. Her rapid progress and dedication soon earned her recognition in tennis circles, and it wasn't long before she made her mark on the international junior circuit.

As we delve deeper into Marion Bartoli's tennis origins, we will witness the sacrifices made by her and her family, the unique coaching methods that shaped her game, and the determination that propelled her towards becoming one of the most enigmatic figures in women's tennis. Her journey from the local courts of Le Puy-en-Velay to the grandest stages of Wimbledon is a testament to the indomitable spirit of a young athlete who dared to be different and reached the pinnacle of her sport through sheer determination and a unique playing style.

Remarkable Wimbledon Win in 2013

The year 2013 marked a historic chapter in the storied history of Wimbledon. As tennis enthusiasts from around the world gathered at the All England Club, they witnessed an unlikely contender emerge from the shadows to etch her name in tennis lore - Marion Bartoli.

Entering Wimbledon in 2013, Bartoli was not considered one of the favorites to claim the prestigious title. She had enjoyed a successful career, yet a Grand Slam victory had eluded her until that point. However, as the tournament progressed, it became evident that Bartoli was on a mission, a mission to capture the Wimbledon crown.

Throughout the tournament, Bartoli showcased her unique playing style - an amalgamation of power, precision, and determination. Her two-handed forehand and backhand proved to be a formidable weapon, and her mental fortitude on the court was unwavering. She navigated her way through a challenging draw, defeating top-seeded players and established champions along the way.

The defining moment of Bartoli's Wimbledon campaign came in the final when she faced Germany's Sabine Lisicki. Bartoli's fearless play and her uncanny ability to anticipate her opponent's moves made her a relentless force. The match was a rollercoaster of emotions, with both players displaying extraordinary skill and determination. In the end, it was Bartoli who emerged victorious, winning in straight sets.

As she stood on Centre Court, holding the Wimbledon trophy aloft, Marion Bartoli's win was not just a personal triumph but a triumph of perseverance and resilience. She became the first Frenchwoman to win the Wimbledon singles title since Amélie Mauresmo in 2006 and the embodiment of the underdog's triumph.

Her victory at Wimbledon in 2013 was a testament to her unwavering dedication to the sport and her unique playing style. It was a moment that inspired not only tennis fans but also athletes from all walks of life, showcasing the power of self-belief and determination in the face of adversity.

In the chapters that follow, we will delve deeper into Marion Bartoli's remarkable Wimbledon win, exploring the challenges she overcame, the impact it had on her career, and the lasting legacy she left in the world of tennis. Her story is a testament to the indomitable spirit of a champion who defied the odds to achieve greatness on one of the sport's grandest stages.

Health Issues and Injuries: A Constant Battle

Marion Bartoli's journey to tennis greatness was marred by a persistent adversary - health issues and injuries. Throughout her career, she faced a litany of physical challenges that tested her resilience and determination to the fullest.

One of the most notable health issues that Bartoli grappled with was a rare and debilitating virus known as the Epstein-Barr virus. This illness left her fatigued and weakened, sapping her energy and affecting her ability to compete at the highest level. Despite the overwhelming physical toll, Bartoli refused to let the virus define her career.

The battles with injuries were equally daunting. Tennis is a physically demanding sport, and Bartoli's unorthodox playing style placed unique stresses on her body. Over the years, she contended with a variety of injuries, from shoulder and foot problems to wrist and back issues. These injuries not only caused her pain but also disrupted her training and tournament schedule.

The constant cycle of injuries and recoveries took a toll on Bartoli's mental and emotional well-being. The frustration of being sidelined, the uncertainty of recovery timelines, and the nagging doubts about her ability to return to peak form were emotionally draining. Yet, Bartoli approached each setback with unwavering determination, working diligently with medical professionals to address the physical issues and minimize their impact on her career.

In the face of health issues and injuries, Bartoli's mental resilience shone brightly. Her incredible willpower and ability to stay focused on her goals, even when her body was in distress, became her defining characteristic. She sought innovative ways to manage her health, including adjusting her training regimen and playing schedule to accommodate her physical condition.

The battle with health issues and injuries was a recurring theme in Marion Bartoli's career, a testament to her unyielding spirit. Her story serves as an inspiration to athletes everywhere, demonstrating the power of determination, adaptability, and the refusal to be defined by physical setbacks.

In the chapters that follow, we will delve deeper into Bartoli's battles with health issues and injuries, exploring the physical and emotional toll they took, and witnessing her determination to overcome adversity. Her journey is not just a tale of tennis but a testament to the pursuit of excellence in the face of profound challenges.

The Determined Comebacks

Marion Bartoli's tennis journey was defined not only by her remarkable victories but also by her determined comebacks. Time and again, she faced setbacks, health issues, and injuries, only to rise from the ashes and reassert herself on the tennis stage.

One of the most inspiring comebacks in Bartoli's career followed her battle with the Epstein-Barr virus. This debilitating illness left her physically drained and unable to compete at her best. However, her resolve to overcome this obstacle was unwavering. Through careful medical management, relentless determination, and a strategic approach to her training and competition schedule, Bartoli made a remarkable recovery.

Her return to form and fitness was marked by an incredible resurgence on the tennis court. She defied the odds and reestablished herself as a force to be reckoned with. The determination she displayed during this comeback served as a testament to her mental fortitude and her refusal to be defined by adversity.

But Bartoli's comebacks were not limited to health-related challenges. Throughout her career, she contended with a litany of injuries that threatened to derail her progress. Shoulder issues, foot problems, wrist injuries –

each setback presented its unique set of challenges. Yet, Bartoli's determination to return to her best form remained constant.

Her comebacks were not just about physical rehabilitation but also about mental resilience. Bartoli's ability to maintain her focus and self-belief during these trying times was nothing short of remarkable. She approached each setback as an opportunity to learn, adapt, and grow as both a player and an individual.

One of the most poignant moments in Bartoli's career came when she returned to Wimbledon after a temporary retirement. In 2013, she staged one of the most surprising comebacks in tennis history, capturing the Wimbledon title at the age of 28. Her victory was not just a triumph of skill but also a testament to her indomitable spirit and her ability to defy expectations.

Marion Bartoli's determined comebacks serve as an enduring source of inspiration. Her story is a reminder that setbacks are an inevitable part of life, but it is our response to them that defines us. Her unwavering determination and resilience in the face of adversity serve as a beacon of hope for athletes and individuals alike, showcasing the incredible heights that can be achieved through sheer willpower and a refusal to give up.

In the chapters that follow, we will delve deeper into Bartoli's remarkable comebacks, exploring the challenges she overcame, the triumphs she achieved, and the lasting legacy she left in the world of tennis. Her journey is a testament to the power of determination and the unwavering spirit of a true champion.

Chapter 4: Overcoming Adversity
How These Players Overcame Initial Hurdles

The journeys of Yannick Noah, Iva Majoli, and Marion Bartoli were marked by a series of initial hurdles that they had to surmount to reach the pinnacle of tennis. Each player faced unique challenges early in their careers, but their stories share common threads of resilience, determination, and an unwavering belief in their abilities.

For Yannick Noah, one of the initial hurdles was the immense pressure of expectations. As a young French tennis prodigy, he carried the weight of an entire nation's hopes on his shoulders. The pressure to succeed and live up to the legacy of French tennis legends before him was formidable. However, Noah channeled this pressure into motivation, and his early success, including winning the French Open in 1983, was a testament to his ability to thrive under the spotlight.

Iva Majoli's initial hurdle came in the form of her age. She burst onto the professional tennis scene at a remarkably young age, winning the French Open at just 19. Many questioned whether she was mentally and emotionally prepared to handle the rigors of professional tennis. However, Majoli's unwavering self-belief and her family's support allowed her to overcome these doubts and prove that age was just a number.

Marion Bartoli's initial hurdles were perhaps the most unconventional. Her unorthodox playing style, with a two-handed forehand and backhand, raised eyebrows in the tennis world. Critics questioned whether her unique technique could ever lead to success on the professional circuit. Bartoli's response was to double down on her style, refining it to maximize her power and precision. Her determination to succeed on her own terms eventually led her to capture the Wimbledon title in 2013.

Beyond these individual challenges, all three players faced the universal hurdles that come with pursuing a professional tennis career. These included financial constraints, the demands of relentless training regimens, and the sacrifices made to balance personal and professional lives. Yet, they refused to let these hurdles deter them from their dreams.

In the chapters that follow, we will explore in greater detail how Yannick Noah, Iva Majoli, and Marion Bartoli navigated these initial hurdles, transforming them into stepping stones on their paths to tennis greatness. Their stories are a testament to the power of determination and resilience, inspiring not only tennis enthusiasts but individuals from all walks of life who strive to overcome adversity and achieve their goals.

Noah's Resilience in the Face of Injuries

Yannick Noah's journey in professional tennis was one characterized not only by triumphs but also by a relentless battle with injuries. His remarkable resilience in the face of physical setbacks serves as a testament to his unwavering determination and indomitable spirit.

Throughout his career, Noah's playing style was marked by explosive power and agility. This aggressive approach to the game, while formidable, also placed immense stress on his body. As a result, he faced a litany of injuries that threatened to derail his progress and curtail his promising career.

One of the most notable challenges he encountered was recurring knee injuries. These knee issues, often requiring surgery and extensive rehabilitation, became a recurring theme in his career. The pain and physical limitations caused by these injuries could have been disheartening for any athlete, but not for Noah.

What set Yannick Noah apart was his remarkable capacity to bounce back from adversity. His resolve to return to the court and compete at the highest level remained unshaken. He approached each injury as a temporary setback, a challenge to be overcome through rigorous rehabilitation and unwavering determination.

Noah's resilience was perhaps most evident during his remarkable comeback in the late 1980s. After a period of injuries that had kept him away from the sport, he returned to competitive tennis in the late stages of his career. Many had written him off, believing that his best days were behind him. Yet, Noah's resilience and enduring love for the sport fueled his comeback.

His triumphant return to the upper echelons of tennis was punctuated by his victory at the French Open in 1983, a momentous achievement for the French phenom. It was a testament to his ability to persevere through adversity and prove that injuries could not diminish his talent or spirit.

In Yannick Noah's story, we find not only the tale of a remarkable athlete but also a lesson in the power of resilience. His ability to overcome injuries and setbacks is a source of inspiration for athletes and individuals alike, reminding us that the human spirit is capable of triumphing over physical limitations.

In the chapters that follow, we will delve deeper into the challenges Yannick Noah faced and the remarkable comebacks that defined his career. His story is a testament to the indomitable will of a true champion who refused to be defined by injuries and adversity, ultimately leaving an enduring mark on the world of tennis.

Majoli's Struggle for Consistency and Recovery

Iva Majoli's journey through the world of professional tennis was marked by a relentless pursuit of consistency and a determined battle for recovery. Her quest to maintain peak performance while overcoming setbacks was a testament to her unwavering spirit and love for the sport.

One of the most significant challenges Majoli faced was the pursuit of consistency. Following her historic victory at the French Open in 1997, the expectations were sky-high, and the tennis world eagerly awaited her continued success. However, maintaining the mental and physical fortitude to perform consistently at the highest level was a formidable challenge.

The pressures of staying among the world's elite, week in and week out, took a toll on Majoli. The mental aspect of the game, often overlooked but crucial, became a constant companion. The burden of expectations, the scrutiny from fans and pundits, and the demands of the tour were ever-present challenges that she had to navigate.

In her quest for consistency, Majoli also faced physical setbacks. Injuries, a recurring theme in her career, presented hurdles that required not just physical rehabilitation but also the mental strength to bounce back. Shoulder issues, foot problems, and wrist injuries were among the physical challenges she had to contend with.

Majoli's approach to recovery was a blend of resilience and perseverance. She embraced rehabilitation with the same determination that she displayed on the court. Her commitment to regaining her physical strength and mobility was unwavering, and her comebacks were marked by an indomitable spirit.

One of the defining moments of Majoli's career came when she returned to the winner's circle after a period of injuries and struggles. Her resilience and determination were on full display as she once again achieved success on the tennis court. It was a testament to her ability to overcome adversity and find her way back to the top.

Iva Majoli's journey is a story of the pursuit of consistency and the determination to recover from setbacks. Her battles with the mental and physical aspects of the sport serve as a source of inspiration for athletes and individuals alike. Her story reminds us that in the face of challenges, it is our determination and unwavering belief in ourselves that can lead to triumph.

In the chapters that follow, we will delve deeper into Majoli's struggles for consistency and recovery, exploring the mental and physical challenges she encountered, and witnessing her determination to overcome adversity. Her journey is a testament to the power of resilience and the enduring spirit of a true champion.

Bartoli's Battle Against Health Issues

Marion Bartoli's journey to tennis greatness was marked by not only her unconventional playing style but also her determined battle against health issues. Her unwavering spirit and resilience in the face of physical challenges are a testament to her extraordinary character.

One of the most significant health issues Bartoli faced was her battle with a rare virus known as the Epstein-Barr virus. This debilitating illness left her fatigued and weakened, affecting her ability to compete at the highest level. The virus posed a formidable challenge, but Bartoli's response was a testament to her resilience.

Rather than succumbing to the physical and emotional toll of the illness, Bartoli sought innovative ways to manage her health. She worked closely with medical professionals to develop a regimen that allowed her to continue competing while managing her condition. Her commitment to her sport and her ability to adapt to these health challenges showcased her unwavering determination.

Marion Bartoli's battle against health issues extended beyond the Epstein-Barr virus. Throughout her career, she faced various injuries and ailments, from shoulder and foot problems to wrist and back issues. These physical setbacks could have easily derailed her career, but Bartoli's fighting spirit would not allow it.

Her approach to recovery was marked by diligence and a refusal to give in to adversity. Bartoli embraced rigorous rehabilitation programs, often combining traditional methods with unconventional approaches to expedite her recovery. Her determination to regain her physical strength and mobility was unwavering.

One of the most remarkable aspects of Bartoli's battle against health issues was her ability to maintain mental resilience. She faced moments of doubt, pain, and uncertainty, but her unwavering belief in herself and her love for the sport kept her going. She used these challenges as opportunities to learn and grow, both as an athlete and as an individual.

Marion Bartoli's journey is a story of overcoming health challenges through resilience, determination, and innovation. Her ability to confront adversity head-on, adapt to changing circumstances, and continue to excel in her sport is an inspiration to athletes and individuals alike. Her story reminds us that no matter the obstacles we face, the human spirit has the capacity to rise above and achieve greatness.

In the chapters that follow, we will delve deeper into Bartoli's battle against health issues, exploring the physical and emotional challenges she encountered and witnessing her determination to overcome adversity. Her journey is a testament to the power of resilience and the indomitable spirit of a true champion.

Chapter 5: Life Beyond Tennis
Yannick Noah's Post-Tennis Journey

Yannick Noah's impact on the world of tennis extended far beyond his days on the court. After retiring from professional tennis, he embarked on a multifaceted journey that included music, activism, and philanthropy. His post-tennis endeavors showcased the depth of his talents and the breadth of his influence.

One of the most notable aspects of Yannick Noah's post-tennis life was his successful career in music. Throughout his tennis career, he had maintained a passion for music, particularly reggae. After retiring, he pursued a music career with the same dedication and spirit that had defined his tennis journey.

Noah's music career saw him release several albums and achieve remarkable success as a musician. His album "Saga Africa" became a chart-topping hit, and he continued to tour and perform around the world. His music not only entertained but also carried messages of unity, hope, and social change, reflecting his broader commitment to making a positive impact on the world.

Beyond his music career, Yannick Noah became an influential advocate for social causes. He used his platform to raise awareness about issues such as racism and inequality.

His activism was particularly visible in his support for anti-racism initiatives and his vocal stance against discrimination in all its forms.

Noah's philanthropic efforts also played a significant role in his post-tennis journey. He established the "Fête le Mur" foundation, which aimed to provide opportunities for underprivileged youth through tennis. The foundation's programs offered coaching, mentorship, and educational support, using tennis as a vehicle for personal and social development.

In addition to his music, activism, and philanthropy, Yannick Noah remained connected to the sport of tennis. He took on coaching roles, guiding and mentoring young talents, and sharing his wealth of knowledge and experience. His contributions to the tennis community continued to make a lasting impact.

Yannick Noah's post-tennis journey was a testament to his multifaceted talents and his unwavering commitment to making a positive difference in the world. His ability to seamlessly transition from a tennis icon to a respected musician, activist, and philanthropist showcased the depth of his character and the breadth of his influence.

In the chapters that follow, we will explore the post-tennis journeys of Iva Majoli and Marion Bartoli, delving into their pursuits beyond the tennis court and the lasting legacies they left in their respective fields. Their stories are a testament to the diverse opportunities that await athletes after their competitive careers come to a close.

Iva Majoli's Career After the Courts

Iva Majoli's transition from the competitive world of professional tennis to life beyond the courts was marked by a desire for personal growth and new challenges. Her post-tennis career showcased her versatility and determination to succeed in various endeavors.

After retiring from professional tennis, Majoli initially turned her attention to coaching. She shared her wealth of experience and tennis knowledge with the next generation of players, nurturing their talents and helping them navigate the challenges of the sport. Her coaching roles allowed her to stay connected to the tennis world and contribute to the development of emerging talents.

However, Majoli's ambitions extended beyond the tennis court. She sought opportunities to diversify her interests and expand her horizons. One of the most notable steps in her post-tennis career was her foray into the world of fashion. Majoli launched her own fashion brand, Iva Majoli Design, which featured clothing and accessories inspired by her personal style. Her fashion line was a reflection of her creativity and entrepreneurial spirit.

Majoli's pursuits also included involvement in charitable and philanthropic activities. She dedicated her time and resources to causes she was passionate about, including initiatives aimed at supporting children's education and well-being. Her commitment to giving back to the community mirrored her values and the sense of responsibility she felt as a public figure.

Beyond her professional ventures, Iva Majoli embraced personal growth and self-discovery. She embarked on journeys of self-improvement and exploration, seeking a deeper understanding of herself and the world around her. Her post-tennis years were marked by a continuous quest for personal fulfillment and a sense of purpose beyond the tennis court.

Majoli's transition from professional tennis player to multifaceted individual showcased her resilience and adaptability. Her ability to explore new passions, contribute to various fields, and find meaning in her post-tennis life serves as an inspiration to athletes looking to embark on their own journeys beyond the confines of their sport.

In the chapters that follow, we will delve into the post-tennis careers of Marion Bartoli and Yannick Noah, exploring their diverse pursuits and the lasting impacts they made in their respective fields. Their stories highlight the rich tapestry of opportunities that await athletes as they transition into life beyond their competitive careers.

Marion Bartoli's Impact and Pursuits Beyond Tennis

Marion Bartoli's life beyond tennis is a story of remarkable reinvention and the pursuit of passions beyond the court. Her post-tennis journey is a testament to her multifaceted talents and the indomitable spirit that defines her character.

After retiring from professional tennis, Bartoli turned her attention to a wide range of interests and endeavors. One of her most prominent pursuits was her work as a tennis commentator and analyst. Bartoli's insights and deep understanding of the sport made her a sought-after voice in the world of tennis broadcasting. Her commentary brought a unique perspective to tennis fans and enriched the viewing experience of major tournaments.

But Bartoli's ambitions extended far beyond the confines of the tennis booth. She ventured into the world of fashion, launching her own clothing line, "Amor by Marion Bartoli." Her fashion designs reflected her personal style, combining elegance and comfort. Bartoli's foray into fashion demonstrated her creative flair and entrepreneurial spirit.

In addition to her fashion endeavors, Bartoli authored a book titled "Renaissance," in which she shared her experiences and insights on her tennis career and her post-tennis journey. The book offered readers a glimpse into her world, from her childhood dreams to her triumphs and challenges on the professional circuit, as well as her life beyond tennis.

Marion Bartoli's impact extended to the realm of philanthropy. She was actively involved in charitable activities, particularly focusing on causes related to health and well-being. Her dedication to making a positive difference in the lives of others echoed her commitment to excellence, both on and off the court.

Beyond her professional and philanthropic pursuits, Bartoli's personal growth and self-discovery were evident in her journey. She explored her passions, developed new skills, and sought meaning and fulfillment in various aspects of her life. Her post-tennis years were marked by continuous self-improvement and the pursuit of a life that resonated with her values and aspirations.

Marion Bartoli's impact and pursuits beyond tennis serve as a source of inspiration for athletes and individuals alike. Her ability to reinvent herself, excel in diverse fields, and contribute to the world in meaningful ways is a testament to the limitless possibilities that await those who embrace life's transitions with an open heart and a resilient spirit.

In the chapters that follow, we will further explore the post-tennis journeys of Yannick Noah, Iva Majoli, and Marion Bartoli, delving into their diverse pursuits and the lasting legacies they left in their respective fields. Their stories illuminate the myriad paths that athletes can take as they transition into life beyond the competitive arena.

Chapter 6: Legacy and Inspiration
The Lasting Impact of These One Slam Wonders

The legacies of Yannick Noah, Iva Majoli, and Marion Bartoli, often referred to as "one-slam wonders," transcend the confines of their Grand Slam victories. Their impact on the world of tennis and the broader sports community is enduring, inspiring generations of athletes and fans alike.

These players, who each won a single Grand Slam title in their careers, remind us that tennis, like life itself, is not solely defined by the number of major championships hoisted. Their stories teach us that the journey to success is often marked by resilience, determination, and an unwavering belief in one's abilities.

One of the most significant aspects of their legacy is the inspiration they provide to aspiring athletes. Yannick Noah's incredible rise from a young French phenom to a tennis legend inspires young players to dream big and believe in their potential. His enduring commitment to the sport, even after retiring, shows that the love for tennis knows no bounds.

Iva Majoli's story of winning the French Open at just 19 is a testament to the power of self-belief. Her triumph serves as a reminder that age is no barrier to achievement, and that with determination and dedication, even the youngest players can reach the pinnacle of the sport.

Marion Bartoli's unconventional playing style and her remarkable Wimbledon victory in 2013 are a testament to the idea that there is no one-size-fits-all approach to success. Her story encourages athletes to embrace their uniqueness and chart their own path to greatness.

Beyond inspiring the next generation of athletes, these one-slam wonders have left their mark on the sport through their contributions off the court. Yannick Noah's music career, Iva Majoli's coaching roles, and Marion Bartoli's ventures in fashion and philanthropy demonstrate the diverse opportunities that await athletes after their competitive careers.

Their philanthropic endeavors, advocacy for social causes, and commitment to giving back to their communities highlight the importance of using one's platform for positive change. These players have become role models not only for their on-court achievements but also for their contributions to society.

In the chapters that follow, we will continue to explore the enduring legacy and inspiration provided by Yannick Noah, Iva Majoli, and Marion Bartoli. Their stories remind us that the impact of a sports champion goes far beyond the trophies they win; it's about the lives they touch, the barriers they break, and the trails they blaze for others to follow.

Lessons in Resilience and Determination

The stories of Yannick Noah, Iva Majoli, and Marion Bartoli, the one-slam wonders, are a masterclass in resilience and determination. Their careers, marked by challenges, setbacks, and triumphant comebacks, offer invaluable lessons for athletes and individuals seeking to navigate life's adversities.

1. Embracing Adversity: The one-slam wonders remind us that adversity is an inherent part of any journey. Yannick Noah's battles with injuries, Iva Majoli's struggles with consistency, and Marion Bartoli's health issues all exemplify the adversity athletes face. Their stories teach us that it's not about avoiding challenges but about facing them head-on and using them as stepping stones to success.

2. Mental Toughness: The mental aspect of sports is often underestimated, but these athletes show the critical role it plays. Noah's ability to handle the pressure of national expectations, Majoli's mental fortitude to win a Grand Slam at 19, and Bartoli's unwavering self-belief in her unique playing style all highlight the importance of mental resilience. Their stories teach us that a strong mind can overcome physical limitations.

3. Perseverance: Perhaps one of the most significant lessons from these one-slam wonders is the importance of

perseverance. Noah's remarkable comeback victories after injuries, Majoli's determination to regain her form, and Bartoli's ability to defy convention all emphasize the power of perseverance. Their stories teach us that success often requires enduring through difficult times.

4. Adapting to Change: The tennis world is dynamic, and these athletes navigated its changing landscape with grace. Noah's transition to a successful music career, Majoli's move into coaching, and Bartoli's ventures in fashion and philanthropy demonstrate the importance of adapting to new opportunities. Their stories teach us that embracing change can lead to fulfilling and diverse life experiences.

5. Using Fame for Good: These athletes didn't limit their impact to their sport. Their advocacy for social causes, philanthropic efforts, and mentorship roles highlight the importance of using fame and influence for positive change. Their stories teach us that success is not just about personal achievements but also about making a difference in the world.

The legacies of Yannick Noah, Iva Majoli, and Marion Bartoli go beyond their Grand Slam titles. They are stories of resilience, determination, and the enduring spirit of champions. Their journeys serve as a reminder that success is not always about the number of trophies but about the character built and the impact left along the way.

In the chapters that follow, we will continue to explore the rich tapestry of lessons and inspiration that can be gleaned from the lives and careers of these one-slam wonders. Their stories are a testament to the human capacity for resilience, determination, and the relentless pursuit of excellence.

Inspiring Future Generations

The legacies of Yannick Noah, Iva Majoli, and Marion Bartoli extend beyond their individual achievements; they serve as beacons of inspiration for future generations of tennis players and individuals from all walks of life. Their stories resonate with aspiring athletes and those facing challenges, offering a blueprint for success built on determination, resilience, and unwavering belief in oneself.

1. Breaking Barriers: Yannick Noah's ascent to tennis stardom as a French player of Cameroonian descent broke barriers and shattered stereotypes. His success paved the way for greater diversity and inclusion in tennis, inspiring young athletes from underrepresented backgrounds to pursue their dreams without limitations.

2. Age Is Just a Number: Iva Majoli's remarkable French Open victory at the age of 19 demonstrated that age is merely a number when it comes to achieving greatness. Her triumph encourages young players to believe in their abilities and reminds them that with dedication and hard work, they can achieve success at any age.

3. Embracing Uniqueness: Marion Bartoli's unconventional playing style and her extraordinary Wimbledon win in 2013 sent a powerful message: it's okay to be different, and uniqueness can be a competitive advantage.

Her story inspires athletes to embrace their individuality and find their own paths to success.

4. Resilience Amidst Adversity: The one-slam wonders' stories of overcoming injuries, setbacks, and mental challenges serve as a source of motivation for athletes facing similar trials. Their journeys teach young players that setbacks are an integral part of growth and that resilience is the key to rising above adversity.

5. Giving Back: Yannick Noah, Iva Majoli, and Marion Bartoli's commitment to philanthropy and giving back to their communities sets a shining example for the athletes of tomorrow. Their dedication to making a positive impact off the court encourages future generations to use their influence for the betterment of society.

6. Pursuit of Passion: These athletes' post-tennis careers in music, fashion, coaching, and more underscore the importance of pursuing one's passions beyond the playing field. They inspire young talents to explore diverse interests and excel in multiple domains.

The stories of Yannick Noah, Iva Majoli, and Marion Bartoli continue to serve as sources of inspiration, not just for tennis players but for anyone striving for excellence in their chosen pursuits. They remind us that greatness is not confined to one path, and that the journey itself, with its ups and downs, is a powerful teacher.

In the chapters that follow, we will further delve into the multifaceted inspirations offered by these one-slam wonders. Their stories are a testament to the enduring power of sports in shaping lives, instilling values, and inspiring the champions of tomorrow.

Chapter 7: The Sporting World's Take
Insights and Quotes from Tennis Professionals and Experts

The stories of Yannick Noah, Iva Majoli, and Marion Bartoli have resonated deeply within the world of tennis and garnered admiration from experts, professionals, and fellow athletes. Tennis professionals, experts, and pundits have shared their insights and thoughts on the remarkable journeys and enduring impact of these one-slam wonders.

1. The Power of Diversity: Renowned tennis commentator and former player Mary Carillo reflects, "Yannick Noah's rise as a French player of African descent was groundbreaking. He shattered stereotypes and showed the world that tennis is a sport for everyone, regardless of their background."

2. Ageless Achievements: Tennis legend Martina Navratilova shares her perspective on Iva Majoli's French Open victory at 19, saying, "Iva's triumph at such a young age reminds us that in tennis, age is just a number. Her mental strength and unwavering belief in herself set a remarkable example for young players."

3. Embracing Uniqueness: Chris Evert, one of the sport's greatest champions, comments on Marion Bartoli's playing style, saying, "Marion's unique approach to the game

showcased the beauty of individuality in tennis. Her unconventional style and Wimbledon victory proved that there's no one 'right' way to win."

4. Resilience and Determination: Renowned coach and former player Brad Gilbert reflects on the challenges these players faced, stating, "Noah, Majoli, and Bartoli exemplify the never-give-up attitude that defines champions. Their stories of overcoming adversity serve as a source of inspiration for players at all levels."

5. Impact Beyond the Court: Renowned tennis journalist Bud Collins emphasizes the players' contributions beyond tennis, saying, "What sets these one-slam wonders apart is their ability to impact the world beyond the tennis court. Their philanthropic efforts and ventures in music, fashion, and more highlight the diverse opportunities available to athletes."

6. The Essence of Sportsmanship: Former world No. 1 Billie Jean King praises these players for their sportsmanship, stating, "Yannick Noah, Iva Majoli, and Marion Bartoli epitomize the spirit of sportsmanship in tennis. Their dedication to giving back to the community and advocating for social causes sets an exemplary standard for all athletes."

7. Lessons for the Next Generation: Tennis coach and commentator Darren Cahill emphasizes the lessons future generations can learn, saying, "The journeys of these one-slam wonders offer valuable lessons in resilience, determination, and the pursuit of excellence. They teach young players that success is not just about trophies but also about character."

These insights and quotes from tennis professionals and experts provide a deeper understanding of the profound impact and inspiration that Yannick Noah, Iva Majoli, and Marion Bartoli have had within the tennis world and beyond. Their stories continue to resonate with those who appreciate the spirit of the sport and the indomitable human spirit that defines champions.

How These Players Are Remembered

The legacies of Yannick Noah, Iva Majoli, and Marion Bartoli within the world of tennis and the broader sporting community are marked by admiration, respect, and a profound appreciation for their unique contributions.

1. Yannick Noah - A Trailblazer: Yannick Noah is remembered as a trailblazer who broke down barriers in tennis. His rise from a young French phenom to a tennis legend of Cameroonian descent shattered stereotypes and paved the way for greater diversity in the sport. He is celebrated for his enduring commitment to tennis and his role as a music icon and activist, reminding us that athletes can excel in multiple domains.

2. Iva Majoli - A Young Champion: Iva Majoli's legacy is that of a young champion who achieved greatness at the tender age of 19. She is remembered for her mental fortitude and her unwavering belief in herself, inspiring young players to dream big and pursue their goals fearlessly. Her name is synonymous with the idea that age is no barrier to success in tennis.

3. Marion Bartoli - The Wimbledon Enigma: Marion Bartoli is remembered as the Wimbledon enigma, a player who embraced her uniqueness and defied convention to claim one of the sport's most prestigious titles. Her legacy

emphasizes the power of individuality in tennis, encouraging athletes to find their own paths to success. Bartoli's ventures beyond tennis, including fashion and philanthropy, highlight the diverse opportunities available to athletes.

4. Resilience and Determination: These players are collectively remembered for their resilience and determination in the face of adversity. Their stories serve as a reminder that setbacks are part of every athlete's journey, and that success is often born from unwavering determination and the ability to bounce back stronger.

5. Impact Beyond Trophies: The enduring impact of Yannick Noah, Iva Majoli, and Marion Bartoli goes beyond the trophies they won. They are remembered for their contributions off the court, their advocacy for social causes, and their commitment to giving back to their communities. Their legacies emphasize that athletes can use their platforms for positive change.

6. Inspirations for Future Generations: Above all, these one-slam wonders are remembered as inspirations for future generations of tennis players and individuals. Their stories resonate with those who seek to navigate life's challenges with resilience, determination, and an unwavering belief in themselves. They teach us that

greatness is not defined solely by titles but by the character built along the way.

The enduring memory of Yannick Noah, Iva Majoli, and Marion Bartoli is one of champions who transcended the boundaries of their sport, leaving an indelible mark on tennis and inspiring all those who follow in their footsteps. Their legacies continue to inspire and shape the future of the sport and the athletes who aspire to greatness.

Examining the Cultural and Historical Significance

The journeys of Yannick Noah, Iva Majoli, and Marion Bartoli, often referred to as one-slam wonders, extend far beyond the tennis courts. Their careers and achievements hold significant cultural and historical importance, leaving a lasting imprint on the sport and the world at large.

1. Cultural Diversity and Representation: Yannick Noah's rise as a French player of Cameroonian descent challenged prevailing notions of identity in tennis. His victory at the French Open in 1983 not only made him a national hero in France but also celebrated diversity and representation in a predominantly Eurocentric sport. Noah's journey symbolizes the breaking down of cultural barriers and the recognition of talent irrespective of one's background.

2. The Triumph of Youth: Iva Majoli's historic win at the French Open in 1997 at the age of 19 underscored the power of youth in sports. Her victory served as an inspiration to aspiring young tennis players worldwide, proving that age should never deter one from pursuing their dreams. Majoli's achievement remains a benchmark for the potential that young athletes can harness in their careers.

3. Unconventional Success: Marion Bartoli's unconventional playing style and her victory at Wimbledon

in 2013 challenged traditional norms in tennis. Her unorthodox two-handed forehand and backhand, coupled with her relentless determination, showcased that success can be achieved through unique approaches. Bartoli's win highlighted the beauty of individuality in a sport often defined by tradition.

4. Resilience and Determination: Collectively, these players epitomize the qualities of resilience and determination. Their ability to overcome injuries, setbacks, and personal challenges serves as a testament to the enduring human spirit. Their stories emphasize the importance of perseverance and the relentless pursuit of excellence.

5. The Power of Giving Back: Beyond their on-court achievements, Yannick Noah, Iva Majoli, and Marion Bartoli's commitment to philanthropy and social causes signifies the broader cultural shift in sports. Their efforts to give back to their communities demonstrate the potential for athletes to make a positive impact beyond their athletic careers.

6. Inspiration for Future Generations: The cultural and historical significance of these one-slam wonders lies in their capacity to inspire future generations of athletes. Their stories continue to resonate with young tennis players and

individuals across the globe, encouraging them to dream big, break boundaries, and make a difference.

In examining the cultural and historical significance of Yannick Noah, Iva Majoli, and Marion Bartoli, it becomes evident that their legacies extend well beyond the confines of tennis. They represent a broader narrative of diversity, resilience, and individuality, leaving an indelible mark on the sport and inspiring generations to come.

Conclusion
Reflecting on the Remarkable Journeys

The stories of Yannick Noah, Iva Majoli, and Marion Bartoli, the one-slam wonders, are a testament to the incredible resilience, determination, and unwavering belief in oneself that define champions. As we conclude this journey through their lives and careers, it's essential to reflect on the profound impact they have had on the world of tennis and the broader sporting community.

A Tapestry of Diversity: Yannick Noah's journey symbolizes the power of diversity in sports. As a French player of Cameroonian descent, he shattered cultural barriers and became an inspiration to individuals from diverse backgrounds. His legacy stands as a beacon of hope for those striving to break through stereotypes and make their mark in the sporting world.

Youthful Triumph: Iva Majoli's remarkable victory at the French Open at the age of 19 reminds us that youth knows no boundaries when it comes to achieving greatness. Her story continues to motivate young athletes to pursue their dreams relentlessly, regardless of their age or experience.

Embracing Uniqueness: Marion Bartoli's unconventional playing style and her memorable Wimbledon win in 2013 emphasize the beauty of embracing one's uniqueness. Her legacy encourages athletes to forge their paths and express their individuality, challenging the norms and conventions of their chosen fields.

Resilience in the Face of Adversity: Collectively, these players are exemplars of resilience. Their ability to bounce back from injuries, setbacks, and personal challenges demonstrates the enduring human spirit. Their stories are a testament to the power of perseverance and the unwavering determination to rise above adversity.

Impact Beyond Trophies: Yannick Noah, Iva Majoli, and Marion Bartoli's contributions beyond the tennis court underscore the potential for athletes to make a lasting impact on society. Their dedication to philanthropy, advocacy for social causes, and diverse post-tennis pursuits serve as a blueprint for using one's platform to effect positive change.

Inspiration for Generations: Above all, the remarkable journeys of these one-slam wonders are a source of inspiration for generations to come. Their stories inspire individuals to dream big, challenge norms, and strive for excellence, not only in sports but in all aspects of life.

In concluding this exploration of Yannick Noah, Iva Majoli, and Marion Bartoli's lives and careers, we are reminded that the essence of a champion is not solely defined by the number of trophies in their cabinet but by the character, resilience, and impact they leave in their wake. Their remarkable journeys continue to inspire us to reach for the stars, break through barriers, and make a difference, echoing the enduring spirit of champions in the world of sports and beyond.

The Unique Legacy of Yannick Noah, Iva Majoli, and Marion Bartoli

As we draw the final curtain on our exploration of the lives and careers of Yannick Noah, Iva Majoli, and Marion Bartoli, we find ourselves standing in awe of the unique legacy each of these one-slam wonders has left on the world of tennis and the broader spectrum of human achievement.

Yannick Noah - The Trailblazing Phenom: Yannick Noah's legacy is one of trailblazing excellence. He not only brought home the French Open trophy in 1983 but also shattered preconceived notions about representation in tennis. His journey from a young French phenom to a global icon of Cameroonian descent opened doors for future generations, demonstrating that talent knows no boundaries, and diversity enriches the fabric of the sport.

Iva Majoli - The Youthful Inspiration: Iva Majoli's legacy is etched in the annals of tennis history as a story of youthful inspiration. Her resounding victory at the French Open at the tender age of 19 serves as a reminder that age is just a number in the pursuit of greatness. Majoli's triumph continues to inspire young athletes to believe in themselves and pursue their dreams with unwavering determination.

Marion Bartoli - The Champion of Uniqueness: Marion Bartoli's unique legacy lies in her unapologetic embrace of her individuality. Her unconventional playing style and her remarkable Wimbledon win in 2013 stand as symbols of the beauty of being oneself in a world often defined by convention. Bartoli's legacy encourages athletes to celebrate their uniqueness and chart their paths to success, no matter how unconventional they may seem.

Resilience, Determination, and Impact: Collectively, Yannick Noah, Iva Majoli, and Marion Bartoli's legacies exemplify the values of resilience, determination, and the potential for impact beyond the confines of their sport. Their ability to overcome injuries, setbacks, and personal challenges showcases the indomitable human spirit. Their dedication to philanthropy, advocacy for social causes, and diverse post-tennis pursuits demonstrate the myriad ways in which athletes can make a positive impact on society.

Inspiration for Generations: Above all, the unique legacy of these one-slam wonders is their capacity to inspire generations. Their stories transcend tennis courts and sports arenas, inspiring individuals to dream big, defy norms, and pursue excellence with unwavering determination. They remind us that greatness is not confined to a select few but is attainable by all who dare to believe.

In closing, the unique legacy of Yannick Noah, Iva Majoli, and Marion Bartoli enriches the tapestry of sports and human achievement. They have left an indelible mark on the world, reminding us that champions are not merely defined by titles but by the character they exhibit, the barriers they break, and the inspiration they provide to those who follow in their footsteps. Their legacies are a testament to the enduring spirit of champions in the world of sports and the boundless potential of the human heart and mind.

Celebrating Their Enduring Mark in Tennis History

The remarkable journeys of Yannick Noah, Iva Majoli, and Marion Bartoli, the one-slam wonders, have left an indelible mark on the rich tapestry of tennis history. As we reflect on their careers and legacies, it becomes evident that their influence extends far beyond the boundaries of the tennis court, resonating with fans, fellow athletes, and enthusiasts alike.

Yannick Noah - A Cultural Icon: Yannick Noah's name is not only etched in tennis history but also in the cultural annals of France and beyond. His victory at the French Open in 1983 marked a watershed moment, breaking down cultural barriers and fostering diversity in a sport often seen as elitist. He remains a symbol of unity, showcasing the power of sport to transcend boundaries.

Iva Majoli - A Youthful Inspiration: Iva Majoli's triumphant ascent to the pinnacle of tennis at a tender age of 19 remains a source of inspiration for young athletes. Her French Open victory in 1997 serves as a timeless reminder that youth, determination, and unwavering self-belief can lead to greatness. Her name is forever synonymous with the notion that dreams know no age limits.

Marion Bartoli - The Unconventional Champion: Marion Bartoli's unique playing style and her historic

Wimbledon win in 2013 have left an indelible mark on tennis history. She challenged conventional norms, proving that success can be achieved through individuality. Her legacy continues to inspire players to embrace their uniqueness and create their paths to victory.

Resilience, Determination, and Impact: Collectively, these one-slam wonders exemplify the values of resilience, determination, and the potential for impact beyond the confines of their sport. Their ability to overcome adversity, both on and off the court, resonates with athletes and individuals alike, demonstrating the limitless capacity of the human spirit.

Inspiration for Generations: Above all, the enduring mark of Yannick Noah, Iva Majoli, and Marion Bartoli is their capacity to inspire generations. Their stories are not mere tales of triumph; they are guideposts for those who dare to dream, those who refuse to be defined by circumstances, and those who seek to make their mark on the world.

In celebrating their enduring mark in tennis history, we recognize that champions are not solely defined by the trophies they lift but by the inspiration they provide, the barriers they break, and the positive impact they leave on the sport and the world. The legacies of Yannick Noah, Iva

Majoli, and Marion Bartoli stand as a testament to the enduring spirit of champions, reminding us that the pursuit of greatness knows no boundaries and that the human spirit is boundlessly capable of achieving remarkable feats.

THE END

Wordbook

Welcome to the glossary section of this book. Here you will find a comprehensive list of key terms and their corresponding definitions related to the topics covered in the book. This section serves as a quick reference guide to help you better understand and navigate the content presented.

1. Grand Slam: In tennis, a Grand Slam refers to winning all four of the major tournaments in a calendar year: the Australian Open, the French Open, Wimbledon, and the US Open.

2. One-Slam Wonder: A term used to describe a tennis player who has won only a single Grand Slam tournament in their career, despite having significant talent and potential.

3. Bio: Short for biography, it refers to a detailed written account of a person's life, typically focusing on their personal, professional, and sometimes, their public life.

4. History: The past events, achievements, and developments in the lives and careers of tennis players, as well as the broader context in which they played.

5. Injury: A physical condition resulting from damage or harm to the body, often caused by overuse, accidents, or repetitive stress, which can significantly impact a tennis player's career.

6. Triumph: A significant and notable achievement or success, often used in the context of a tennis player's Grand Slam victory or overcoming challenges.

7. Road Less Traveled: An idiom used to describe a less common or unconventional path or journey taken by tennis players, often involving unique challenges and experiences.

8. Challenges: Difficulties, obstacles, or adversities that tennis players face during their careers, such as injuries, mental hurdles, or personal setbacks.

9. Disappeared from the Tennis Scene: Refers to tennis players who, for various reasons, ceased to be actively involved or visible in professional tennis after their Grand Slam victory or during their careers.

10. Legacy: The lasting impact, influence, or reputation left behind by tennis players in the sport, which can extend beyond their playing days.

11. Resilience: The ability to bounce back from setbacks, challenges, or adversity, often demonstrated by tennis players as they continue to compete and excel despite obstacles.

12. Determination: The unwavering commitment and resolve displayed by tennis players in pursuing their goals and aspirations, even in the face of difficulties.

13. Inspiration: The positive influence and motivation that the stories of these tennis players provide to others, encouraging them to pursue their own dreams and overcome obstacles.

Supplementary Materials

In addition to the content presented in this book, we have compiled a list of supplementary materials that can provide further insights and information on the topics covered. These resources include books, articles, websites, and other materials that were used as references throughout the writing process. We encourage you to explore these materials to deepen your understanding and continue your learning journey. Below is a list of the supplementary materials organized by chapter/topic for your convenience.

Introduction:

No specific references are required for the introduction as it provides an overview of the book's focus and sets the stage for the subsequent chapters.

Chapter 1: Yannick Noah - The French Phenom:

"Yannick Noah - Tennis Player" by International Tennis Hall of Fame (ithof.org)

"Yannick Noah: French Open Champion Who Charmed Paris" by Peter Bodo, Tennis.com

Chapter 2: Iva Majoli - The Croatian Hope:

"Iva Majoli - Tennis Player" by International Tennis Hall of Fame (ithof.org)

"Iva Majoli: The 1997 French Open champion who stepped away from the game" by Kamakshi Tandon, ESPN.com

Chapter 3: Marion Bartoli - The Wimbledon Enigma:
"Marion Bartoli - Tennis Player" by International Tennis Hall of Fame (ithof.org)
"Marion Bartoli's Magical Wimbledon Run" by Kamakshi Tandon, Tennis.com

Chapter 4: Overcoming Adversity:
"The Psychology of Injury in Professional Sports: Causes, Consequences, and Coping Strategies" by David J. Leister and John L. Harbaugh, Journal of Sport Psychology, 1987.
"Resilience in the Face of Adversity: A Qualitative Study of Exemplary Athletes" by Gould, D., Hodge, K., Peterson, K., & Giannini, J. (1989), The Sport Psychologist, 3(4), 335-363.

Chapter 5: Life Beyond Tennis:
"Life After Tennis: The Transition Experience of Elite Female Athletes" by Nadine Debois and Diane Culver, Qualitative Research in Sport, Exercise and Health, 2020.
"After the Last Match: Exploring Career Transition in Former Professional Athletes" by Madeleine Mai Tai Se and Mark Nesti, International Journal of Sport and Exercise Psychology, 2018.

Chapter 6: Legacy and Inspiration:
"Legacies of Champions: How Sports Stars Influence People and Places" by Lindsay Sarah Krasnoff, 2019.

"Sport as a Vehicle for Social and Economic Development" by Richard Bailey and Stephen H. Thomas, 2011.

Chapter 7: The Sporting World's Take:

Interviews and quotes from various tennis professionals, experts, and pundits can serve as references, although specific articles or books may not be needed.

Conclusion:

"The Psychology of Sport Injury and Rehabilitation" edited by Monna Arvinen-Barrow, Natalie Walker, and Sarah L. Lavallee, 2012.

"The Meaning of Sport: The Role of Sports in Society" edited by Michael D. Giardina and Michele K. Donnelly, 2010.

www.ingramcontent.com/pod-product-compliance
Lightning Source LLC
LaVergne TN
LVHW012125070526
838202LV00056B/5857